Images of Modern America

NEW ENGLAND
CANDLEPIN BOWLING

Images of Modern America

NEW ENGLAND CANDLEPIN BOWLING

Susan Mara Bregman
Foreword by Mike Morin

ARCADIA
PUBLISHING

Published by Arcadia Publishing
Charleston, South Carolina

Printed in the United States of America

Library of Congress Control Number: 2020937983

For all general information, please contact Arcadia Publishing:
Telephone 843-853-2070
Fax 843-853-0044
E-mail sales@arcadiapublishing.com
For customer service and orders:
Toll-Free 1-888-313-2665

Visit us on the Internet at www.arcadiapublishing.com

For Susan C. We'll always have Paris.

CONTENTS

Foreword 6

Acknowledgments 7

Introduction 8

1. What's in a Name?: A Description of Candlepin Bowling 11

2. Straight Out of Worcester: A History of the Game 25

3. Names in the Game: People and Places 41

4. Outside the Lanes: Candlepins on Television and Beyond 67

5. Staying in the Game: Candlepin Looks to the Future 81

About the Author 95

FOREWORD

It was a Saturday in late August 1984. The sun-splashed view of Boston from my room at the Royal Sonesta Hotel in Cambridge was breathtaking. I would start my new job as a morning radio host on WZOU-FM soon and needed to find a house for my young family, as I visited from out of town. While waiting for my wife to finish getting ready, I turned the television on. The first place I landed was Channel 5. What I saw stopped me in my tracks.

"What the heck is THAT?" I remember mumbling out loud.

What I saw was foreign to me. As a native Detroiter, I only knew one kind of bowling and could never have imagined that the most exciting bowling adventures of my life were about to begin. Within weeks, I would be smitten by candlepins. There would be no going back to the big-ball game.

While reading this book, I fell in love with the game all over again. Despite spending years as a candlepin bowling television analyst, author, and historian, Susan brought me to places I hadn't been before. And that's the beauty of our game.

Turn around, and there is another story you have not heard. For example, I had no idea that iconic Woburn Bowladrome in Massachusetts was built on a site once known as Nanny Goat Hill. Hundreds of blastings later, and there's the bowling center, still standing where it was built by the Gangi family 80 years ago.

You will love the story Susan shares about Lou Pasquale of Boston Bowl, lying injured on a World War II battlefield, and how those 14 grueling hours led to his commitment to community service, including working with at-risk kids.

Television made candlepin bowling a ratings monster, which, in turn, created local celebrities out of laborers, office workers, and everyday people who never asked to be stars. *New England Candlepin Bowling* takes you to where dreams began and memories were made for over 140 years.

—Mike Morin
Author, *Lunch with Tommy and Stasia*

ACKNOWLEDGMENTS

Thank you to everyone who rolled a few strings with me (and usually beat me in the process), including Andy McClurg; Joelle Stein; Joe Beggan; Tom Cohan; Janet Cohan; the Rohloffs (Nicki, John, Meghan, and Rylie); Anne Quirk; Bill Ballou; and Sarah Moore. Special thanks to Liz Budington and Matt Denker, my road trip buddies who expertly steered while I kept an eye out for those pin-shaped signs.

Thank you to the friends and family who put up with my craziness, especially David Dao, Gloria Leipzig, Richard Bregman, Fern Drillings, and Michael Bregman.

Thank you to the team at Arcadia Publishing, including my editors Caitrin Cunningham and Erin Vosgien, who provided the expert advice that helped shape this book.

Some talented photographers shared their work with me: Liz Budington, Kevin Hong (the man behind the Vintage Alleys Project), Mark Stein, and Tom Marchessault, among them. Your images have made this a better book.

Sherry Sheffield of the Wyoming Historical Society enthusiastically helped a perfect stranger by taking photographs of the only candlepin alley in Ohio. Gary Gillis shared memories of his dad, the inimitable Don Gillis, and John Tobin helped find those elusive Channel 5 photographs. Wendy Essery at the Worcester Historical Museum unearthed wonderful photographs, even as the COVID-19 lockdown clock was ticking. Anne Quirk provided her usual expert editorial guidance. The International Candlepin Bowling Association and the New England Sports Museum shared their archives. Bob Parrella, Maria Angelotti, and fellow author Mike Morin all opened doors for me.

Finally, I could not have written this book without the candlepin community. You were gracious and generous with your time. I am grateful to all of you.

Unfortunately, I could not visit every candlepin house in New England, nor was I able to include everyone I spoke with in this book. For both, I apologize. Writing a book is a balancing act. My goal was to be representative, not exhaustive, and to present an affectionate look at this quirky, challenging, and frustrating game.

I took many of the photographs in this book, and these are credited to the author. WHM indicates photographs from the collection of the Worcester Historical Museum, Worcester, Massachusetts. ICBA identifies images from the International Candlepin Bowling Association. Full credits for all other images are in the text.

INTRODUCTION

Ancient Egyptians and Romans did it. So did Henry VIII, Martin Luther, Babe Ruth, Rip Van Winkle, Fred Flintstone, and "The Dude." It is a rite of passage for presidential candidates. Everybody bowls.

Tenpin is the most common version of the game in the United States, but in parts of New England and eastern Canada, bowling means candlepins. Both games use a ball to knock down 10 pins over 10 frames. But the similarities end there.

Tenpin bowling uses bottle-shaped pins and large balls with three finger holes. Bowlers have two chances per frame to knock down all 10 pins.

Candlepin bowling uses cylindrical pins that are tapered slightly at each end. The balls are smaller than tenpin balls, and they fit in a player's hand. They do not have finger holes. Candlepin players have three turns per frame, and the downed pins are not cleared between rolls.

Candlepin bowling was invented in Worcester, Massachusetts, around 1880 and has not strayed far from its roots. Today, the game is played mostly in New England. Candlepin houses are concentrated in Massachusetts, New Hampshire, and Maine; a few can be found in Vermont. Canadians are also candlepin bowlers, and there are centers in Nova Scotia and New Brunswick.

Candlepin is one of four types of small-ball bowling in the United States and Canada. The other games are duckpins, rubber-band duckpins, and five pins. All were developed around the turn of the 20th century and are still played today.

Full disclosure: I grew up in New York, where tenpin rules. I discovered candlepins when I moved to Boston after college. I wish I could say it was love at first sight, but it was not. I played a game here or there, but for most of my adult life, I was oblivious to bowling in any of its variations.

But one night I got together with a couple of old friends, and we decided to go bowling. Once I laced up a pair of rental shoes and picked up one of those small balls, I was hooked. Much to my chagrin, I was not a good bowler—okay, I was terrible. Even when I tried to sneak in a few extra balls by not pressing the reset button when my turn was over, I could barely knock down any pins.

But that is the beauty of candlepin bowling. There is always room for improvement. A perfect score of 300 points—12 consecutive strikes—is not unknown in tenpin. But in more than a century of play, no one has ever rolled a perfect candlepin game. The highest recorded score in candlepin bowling is 245, which has been achieved only twice.

In fact, the true believers scoff at those who roll 300s in tenpin. With those big balls and fat pins, they say, anyone can achieve perfection with enough practice. The difficulty is a point of pride for candlepinners. A story in *Sports Illustrated* concurred. "Indeed, that frustration may be the game's true appeal," Douglas Campbell wrote. He was profiling Stasia Czernicki, the best woman candlepin bowler in the history of the game (and some say the best of either gender), but he spent some time pondering the appeal of those small balls. "On the one hand it mixes well in the dour, Calvinist blood of purebred Yankees," he added. "And on the other it is the perfect metaphor for life in a mill town or in any dead-end job."

Candlepin bowling emerged from a mill town. Most sources say Justin White, called "Pop," invented the game around 1880. White owned a billiards hall on Pearl Street in downtown Worcester. Looking for new ways to keep his customers entertained, he experimented with different kinds of bowling. After a few false starts, he settled on a game that used pins that were two inches in diameter, tapered at both ends, and a four-inch ball. This variation caught on and put candlepin bowling on the path to the game played today.

John J. Monsey worked for Pop White and is credited with popularizing candlepin bowling and standardizing the game. He was a founder of National Duckpin and Candlepin Congress, which convened in 1906 to regulate all aspects of the game.

From bowling leagues to birthday parties, candlepin bowling is woven into the fabric of New England life. The game was featured on television for decades, which put candlepins on equal footing with the region's professional sports, and the pastime has appeared in movies, novels, and an episode of *The Simpsons*.

Since that disastrous outing with my friends, I have visited dozens of candlepin centers across New England. I bowled at small houses with six or eight lanes tucked away in basements. I played at giant suburban centers with 30-plus lanes, arcades, and state-of-the-art scoring systems. I visited some of the oldest candlepin alleys in New England and some of the newest. I tried my hand at cosmic bowling, which creates light shows on the lanes as music blasts in the background. I encountered every type of scoring system—including the hard-to-find tel-e-score machines—but I came to prefer old-school scorekeeping with paper and pencil. I even played a few games of duckpins for the first time since my undergraduate days in Rhode Island.

I spoke with the men and women who own bowling alleys. Some have been in the business for decades; others are new to the industry. I bowled with a sportswriter who was nearing the conclusion of his quest to bowl at every candlepin house in Massachusetts. I met the man who was first to set the record high candlepin score of 245. I interviewed authors who were generous with their insights, and I connected with photographers who generously shared their work. It has been an honor and a pleasure to meet the people who are keeping this game alive.

I emerged from my research with a slightly sore arm and a deep appreciation for this New England tradition.

I have bowled bad games, to be sure, but I have never had a bad experience in a candlepin house. It is true that, as of this writing, I have not rolled a strike. But that is the beauty of candlepin bowling. There is always room for hope.

One

WHAT'S IN A NAME?
A DESCRIPTION OF
CANDLEPIN BOWLING

Candlepin bowling uses small balls and cylindrical pins that are said to resemble candlesticks. The game was invented in Worcester, Massachusetts, at the end of the 19th century and has been woven into the fabric of New England life for 140 years. The game is tough, but so are the players. This is New England, after all.

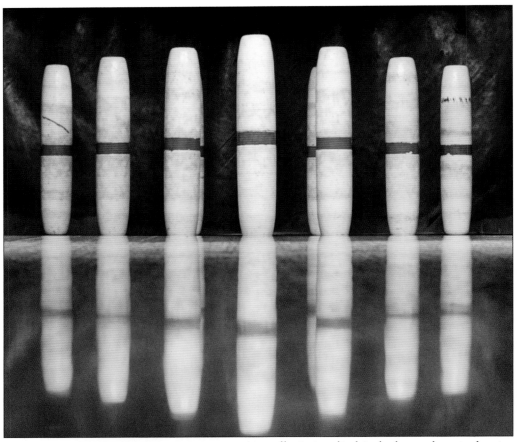

A candlepin is cylindrical, almost three inches in diameter at the widest point, and tapered slightly at each end. Candlepins stand 15.75 inches tall, making them almost an inch taller than a regulation tenpin. The pins are symmetrical, with no distinct top or bottom. (Photograph by author.)

Candlepin balls are four and one-half inches in diameter, about the size of a grapefruit, and they can weigh no more than two pounds, seven ounces. The balls do not have finger holes, and as most bowlers can attest, candlepin balls are small enough to take out a single pin without touching its neighbors. (Photograph by Elizabeth Budington.)

Candlepin uses 10 pins, which are set to form a triangle. Four pins are in the back row, then three and two pins, with one pin, known as the headpin, in front. The pins are set 12 inches apart. They are numbered, with the headpin as No. 1 and then left to right in each row. Here, the ball return at Riverwalk Lanes in Amesbury, Massachusetts, displays the pin numbers. (Photograph by author.)

Candlepin instructors recommend a three-step approach to deliver the ball. For right-handed bowlers, the approach starts with the left foot and ends with a slide, a crouch, and the all-important follow-through. Here, two unidentified bowlers show off their form. (Courtesy of ICBA.)

Like tenpin, a game of candlepin has 10 frames. The games are often called "strings," and the frames are known as "boxes." Because candlepin is harder than tenpin, players have three turns per frame. Downed pins, called "wood," are not cleared between rolls, which adds an element of skill—and chance—as the players try to use the fallen pins to their advantage. "Deadwood" refers to fallen pins that are not playable. A pin is considered dead if it falls into the gutter or lands on the player's side of the deadwood line, which is 24 inches in front of the headpin. Deadwood in the lane is removed before play resumes, but deadwood in the gutter is left in place. Members of the State Mutual candlepin bowling team ponder the fallen pins in 1960. (Courtesy of WHM.)

A candlepin lane consists of an approach area, the lane itself, left and right gutters, and the pin deck. A foul line separates the approach from the lane proper. The approach is 14–16 feet long, and the lane measures 60 feet from the foul line to the center of the headpin. Lanes are 42 inches wide. A player may not cross the foul line when delivering the ball. Candlepin lanes also have a "lob line" 10 feet from the foul line to ensure that players roll the ball instead of throwing it. Any ball that does not touch the lane before crossing the lob line is considered foul. Signs posted at Central Park Lanes in East Boston (above) and Riverwalk Lanes in Amesbury (right), both in Massachusetts, remind players to observe the rules. (Both, photograph by author.)

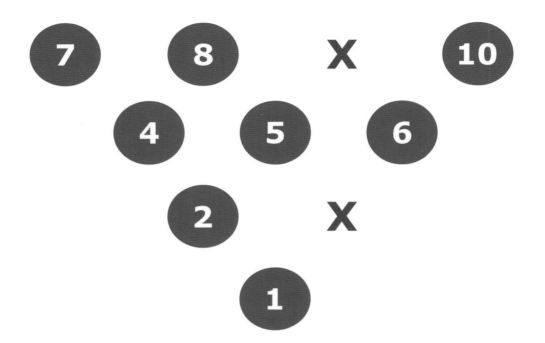

Candlepin bowling has its own vocabulary when it comes to naming the pins left standing. A Half Worcester is the most unusual term and, arguably, the best known. This pattern results when the first ball punches out the 2-8 pins or the 3-9 pins and leaves the rest standing. Industry lore traces the term to a Massachusetts tournament in the 1940s. When a member of the Worcester team knocked out just two pins late in the competition, a member of the other team threw a little shade by saying, "You're halfway back to Worcester." The term has multiple variations, including Half Worcester Left (2-8 pins fall), Half Worcester Right (3-9), Full Worcester (2-3-8-9), and Quarter Worcester (2-pin or 3-pin). Shown here is the Half Worcester Right. (Photograph by author.)

Candlepin bowling lanes were traditionally made from strips of rock maple. Wooden lanes are durable, but they take a beating and require periodic sanding and refinishing. Eventually, the wood wears away, and as a result, many candlepin houses have transitioned to synthetic lanes. The new material requires minimal maintenance, but experienced players say the play action and the sounds of the game are not the same. (Photograph by author.)

Knocking down pins is noisy work, even on synthetic lanes, and many bowling centers use carpeting on the walls to muffle the sound. The carpeting often incorporated the name of the location, like this example at the Big 20 Bowling Center in Scarborough, Maine. (Photograph by author.)

Early bowling alleys were often associated with pool halls and saloons. Florence E. Greenleaf described these seedy origins in *The Game of Candlepin Bowling.* "They were tough places, and they were rough places," she wrote. "They were dirty, poorly lit establishments." Smith's Billiards in Springfield was among the Massachusetts establishments that offered both pool and candlepin bowling. (Photograph by author.)

This rough history may explain why the game developed rules of etiquette. Greenleaf reminded players to stay cool. "Avoid the use of profane language," she wrote. "The pins are inanimate objects and cannot hear your curses." Some proprietors reinforce this advice by posting helpful signs for their patrons. (Photograph by author.)

Perhaps because of the game's sketchy past, many in the industry are trying to take candlepin terminology out of the back streets. Some prefer bowling "centers" to "alleys" and consider "channel" to be a tasteful alternative to "gutter." The French King Bowling Center in Erving, Massachusetts, is one of many candlepin houses calling itself a bowling center. (Photograph by author.)

The grandiose names of many bowling centers follow the mid-century linguistic practice that attached "a-drome" and "a-rama" to everything from hot dog joints to laundromats. To name just a few, Massachusetts is home to "bowladromes" in Wakefield, Woburn, Acton, and Northborough, while "bowl-o-ramas" and "bowl-a-ramas" pop up in Portsmouth, New Hampshire, and Sanford, Maine. Shown here is the former Malden Bowladrome in Malden, Massachusetts. (Photograph by author.)

Why are bowling shoes slippery? It is all about the slide. Smooth soles allow bowlers to glide as they release the ball, ensuring a proper delivery. Competitive bowling shoes have a sliding sole on one foot and a rubber heel on the other to optimize sliding and braking action, respectively. Rental shoes have smooth soles on both feet. (Photograph by author.)

Why are bowling shoes ugly? Some say the unique look of bowling shoes—with the size prominently displayed on the heel—is designed to discourage patrons from stealing the footwear. That does not always work, however, as the *Wall Street Journal* reported in 2001. Bowling shoes had become "cheap chic," and players were liberating them to wear outside the lanes. (Photograph by author.)

Bowling is not just for civilians. Here, an unidentified Marine gets ready to roll at the Marine Corps Schools in Quantico, Virginia. The ball is definitely small, but it is impossible to know whether the service member was rolling duckpins or candlepins from the picture. The mid-Atlantic location suggests the former, but the story may be lost to history. (Courtesy of Marine Corps Photographic Section.)

Other than the requisite shoes, candlepin bowling has no official dress code. However, there has been no shortage of advice over the years, especially for women. In the pamphlet *Candlepin Bowling for Physical Education, Camping and Recreation Programs*, James J. McLaughlin wrote, "Bowling dresses come in attractive one-piece outfits designed especially for the game." An unidentified woman defies that guidance by wearing stylish trousers on the lanes. (Courtesy of ICBA.)

Some candlepin houses still use paper-and-pencil scoresheets. At York Beach Bowling in Maine, customers tear a scoresheet off a wall-mounted pad. Other centers have introduced technology into the process of keeping score. With semiautomatic scoring, players track their downed pins and enter the total into a keypad after each turn. The system does the math, and a scoresheet is displayed on an overhead monitor. (Photograph by Mark H. Stein.)

Players press a button—or occasionally step on a foot pedal—at the conclusion of each box to clear and reset the pins. Shown here is a pair of reset buttons at Bolo's Kitchen, Cantina, and Candlepin in Brunswick, Maine. (Photograph by author.)

Tel-e-score systems consist of a table with a built-in overhead projector. Players use a wax marker to enter their score on a reusable plastic sheet, and results are projected onto a screen. Many centers reserved tele-e-score use for league play and provided paper scoresheets for open bowling. Here is a detail of the tel-e-score at Bolo's Kitchen, Cantina, and Candlepin in Brunswick, Maine. (Photograph by author.)

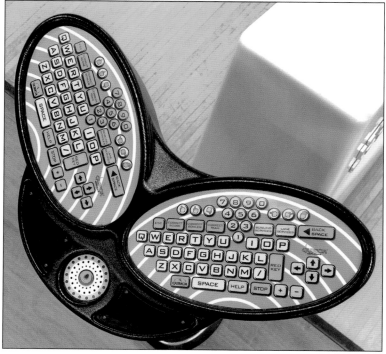

Fully automatic scoring systems track the pinfall, ball by ball, and then reset the pins. Overhead screens display the score—and sometimes the speed of the ball—and animation celebrates high scores and cheerfully chides players for rolling a gutter ball. Shown here is the scoring set-up at Cape Ann Lanes in Gloucester, Massachusetts. (Photograph by Elizabeth Budington.)

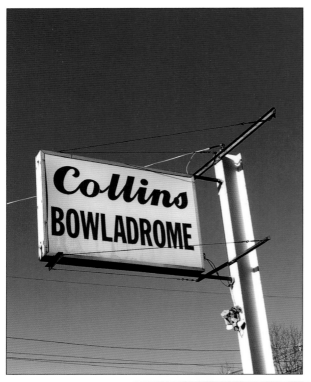

Candlepin is one of four types of small-ball bowling in the United States and Canada. Duckpin uses 10 squat bottle-shaped pins and is played primarily in the mid-Atlantic and southern New England states. The game likely originated around 1900 in Baltimore, Maryland. A variant adds a rubber ring around the pins to improve scoring. Introduced in Pittsburgh, Pennsylvania, in 1905, rubber-band duckpin is now played almost exclusively in Quebec, where it is known as *petites quilles*. Five-pin bowling was developed around 1909 in Toronto, Ontario, and remains a Canadian game. Halfway in size between duckpins and tenpins and outfitted with a rubber band, five pins are set in a V formation. Unlike other small-ball games, each pin is assigned a different point value. Collins Bowladrome is an old-school duckpin house in North Billerica, Massachusetts. (Both, photograph by author.)

Two

STRAIGHT OUT OF WORCESTER
A HISTORY OF THE GAME

Candlepin bowling has deep roots in Massachusetts, and two Bay State men are credited with developing and popularizing the game. Justin "Pop" White owned a bowling and billiards parlor in Worcester, and John J. Monsey was a pool player with a gift for promotion. Working together in the last decades of the 19th century, they developed the game of candlepin bowling as it is played today.

Justin "Pop" White moved from Jamaica, Vermont, to Worcester, Massachusetts, in 1859. Twenty years later, he bought a pool and bowling establishment on Pearl Street. He experimented with different forms of bowling in hopes of finding a more challenging game for his customers. For his first attempt, he found some wooden dowels in his new place and reimagined them as bowling pins. With a diameter of just one inch, the pins were too difficult to knock down. So, White went back to the drawing board and designed pins that were two inches across in the center and tapered to one inch at each end. The new game proved popular, and White began to promote this early version of candlepin bowling throughout the Northeast. Here are Justin White (left) and John Monsey (right) around 1900. (Courtesy of ICBA.)

John J. Monsey, known as Jack, was an itinerant pool player originally from South Hadley, Massachusetts. In 1888, he gave a billiards demonstration at Justin White's establishment, and the 21-year-old was hired on the spot. In *The Game of Candlepin Bowling*, Florence E. Greenleaf described Monsey as "imbued with promotional and organizational skills," and Monsey put his talents to good use. "Jack Monsey absorbed everything 'Pop' White could teach him about bowling and the bowling alley business," Greenleaf wrote. Together, the pair worked to modify and popularize White's game, and by 1893, they had developed the game of candlepin bowling as it is known today. Here, Jack Monsey is shown bowling around 1945. (Courtesy of ICBA.)

ANNUAL BOWLING LEAGUE
BANQUET
WORCESTER PRESSED STEEL.
HOTEL ESSEX — BOSTON, MASS.
APRIL 10th, 1937.

Bowling at the end of the 19th century operated under a "welter of hodge-podge conditions," as Florence E. Greenleaf wrote in *The Game of Candlepin Bowling*. Tenpin, sometimes called "bottlepin," was gaining traction, and the American Bowling Congress was formed to standardize and promote the game. The small-ball games had no comparable structure or oversight, so Jack Monsey and his partners established the National Duckpin and Candlepin Congress. Convening

in Worcester in 1906, the congress codified all aspects of candlepin bowling. The size and shape of the pins were defined, and playing the wood became standard practice. With a set of rules in place, it became possible for leagues to form and players to bowl under consistent conditions. Shown here is the 1937 annual bowling banquet for the Worcester Pressed Steel team. (Courtesy of WHM.)

Early bowling teams had colorful names like Daffodils, Speed Boys, Skidoos, and Cardinals (shown here in 1936). Newspapers of the time covered competitive matches, and scribes had a seemingly endless vocabulary to describe candlepin bowlers, including "pin topplers" and "knights of the thin pins." Writers were not shy about offering advice. In 1912, a publication touting the world champion Worcester team offered "A Few Don'ts." The list included guidance about perseverance that still applies a century later: "Don't quit bowling on account of a sore finger. You have other fingers on the same hand." The members of the Cardinals are, from left to right, (seated) Joseph F. Edwards, Ben Clancy, and Frank Richards; (standing) Dr. William Clancy and attorney William Moore. (Courtesy of the Paul E. Curran Historical Collection, Milford Town Library.)

Before automation, bowling alleys hired "pin boys" or "pinsetters." Stationed at the end of the lane, teenagers or younger children, almost always boys, returned the balls and reset the pins between frames. Quick reflexes were a must, as pinsetters had to dodge errant balls and flying pins, and the hours were long. Working for the National Child Labor Committee (NCLC), investigative photographer Lewis Hine documented child labor practices at the turn of the 20th century. He photographed children as young as five years old working in textile factories, sardine canneries, tobacco fields, and bowling alleys. In 1910, Hine photographed two unnamed youths holding candlepins outside Bowling Academy in Burlington, Vermont. (Photograph by Lewis Wickes Hine; courtesy of the National Child Labor Committee Collection, Library of Congress, Prints and Photographs Division.)

The advocacy of Lewis Hine and the NCLC led to legal protections for the youngest child workers. But teenagers continued to set pins until automation started to put them out of work in the 1950s. Howard M. Dowd and R. Lionel Barrows were partly responsible. In the late 1940s, the pair of attorneys founded the Bowl-Mor Company to manufacture automatic candlepin-setting machines. (Courtesy of WHM.)

Four prototype Bowl-Mor pinsetters were installed at Whalom Park, a now-closed amusement park in Lunenburg, Massachusetts, in 1949. Bowl-Mor went on to dominate the candlepin pinsetting industry until the company folded in the 1960s. Many Bowl-Mor machines are still operating today but often with refurbished or replica parts. An industry flyer promotes the Bowl-Mor Series E candlepin setter. (Courtesy of ICBA.)

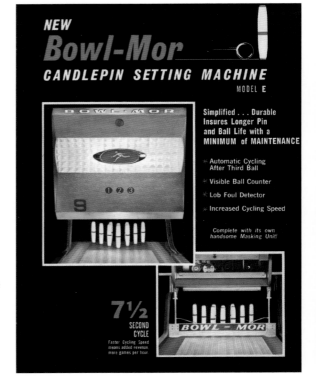

Joseph Janes patented a candlepin-setting machine in the 1950s. The first Janes models were said to be installed in Massachusetts at Turnpike Bowladrome in Cambridge and Holyoke Bowladrome in Holyoke. A detail from the Janes patent application shows part of the mechanism. (Courtesy of US Patent and Trademark Office.)

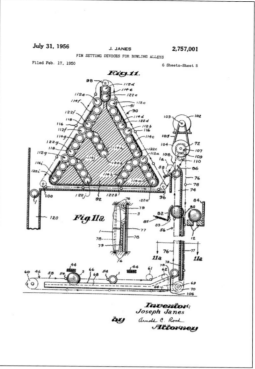

Working in an empty turkey house on a farm in Pearl River, New York, an engineer named Fred Schmidt developed a pinsetter for tenpin bowling in 1936. AMF bought Schmidt's patent—after Brunswick said no—and started selling its pinsetters in 1952. Brunswick followed suit a few years later. Boston Bowl in Dorchester, Massachusetts, which offers tenpin and candlepin bowling, uses QubicaAMF pinsetters for both games. A detail from the tenpin model is shown here. (Photograph by Elizabeth Budington.)

Factories, white-collar businesses, religious institutions, and social organizations sponsored bowling leagues through much of the 20th century. From the 1950s through the 1980s, leagues filled the lanes, often until the wee hours, and candlepin centers relied on this steady traffic to pay the bills. (Courtesy of WHM.)

Today, most leagues are not associated with companies. "One thing I have always loved about league bowling is how it brings together people from all walks of life," said bowler and photographer Kevin Hong. "The members of one team may have nothing in common other than a love for the sport (or hatred of that 10-pin, depending on how you look at it)." Members of two Worcester bowling teams pose for the camera in the 1960s: Gilrein's Steak House (top) and State Mutual. (Courtesy of WHM.)

John Brunswick emigrated from Switzerland to the United States in 1845. He set up a carriage-making shop in Cincinnati, Ohio, but soon started making billiard tables. Brunswick's company merged with two competitors in the 1870s and became the Brunswick-Balke-Collender Company. In 1890, the company began to make wooden bowling lanes, pins, and balls, as shown in this old advertisement, complete with a typo. (Courtesy of ICBA.)

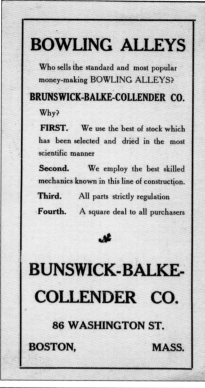

BOWLING ALLEYS

Who sells the standard and most popular money-making BOWLING ALLEYS?

BRUNSWICK-BALKE-COLLENDER CO.

Why?

FIRST. We use the best of stock which has been selected and dried in the most scientific manner

Second. We employ the best skilled mechanics known in this line of construction.

Third. All parts strictly regulation

Fourth. A square deal to all purchasers

BUNSWICK-BALKE-COLLENDER CO.

86 WASHINGTON ST.

BOSTON,   MASS.

Although much of Brunswick's bowling business centered on the tenpin industry, many candlepin houses, including Wakefield Bowladrome, shown here, have equipment bearing the familiar crown logo. The company, by then called Brunswick Corporation, left the bowling business in 2014 and sold 85 retail centers to Bowlmor AMF. A year later, Brunswick sold its bowling products division to a private investment firm. Equipment is still sold under the Brunswick name. (Photograph by author.)

American Machine and Foundry was formed in 1900 by North Carolina businessman Rufus Lenoir Patterson Jr. The company was originally a subsidiary of the American Tobacco Company but was spun off in 1912 with Patterson at the helm. The company entered the bowling business after World War II and began to sell a pinsetter (based on Fred Schmidt's invention) in 1952. (Courtesy of ICBA.)

By the 1970s, AMF manufactured a wide range of recreation equipment, but business reverses forced the company to sell off its bowling business in 1985. A series of mergers, bankruptcies, and reorganizations followed, and today, Bowlero Corporation (formerly Bowlmor AMF) and QubicaAMF Worldwide continue the AMF legacy. On this page, some politically incorrect promotional photographs showcase AMF equipment, probably in the 1960s. (Courtesy of ICBA.)

The Brunswick-Balke-Collender Company patented a ball return system in 1935. The mechanism transported the ball from the pit to the top of an inclined ramp, where gravity and momentum took over to deliver the ball along a return way to the player's end of the lane. Inventor Ernest Hedenskoog described the device as "simple in construction, effective in operation and not at all likely to get out of order." Early ball returns located the return track above the lanes, like these Brunswick models at Needham Bowlaway in Needham, Massachusetts (above). Newer models placed the return path beneath the lanes, like those at Park Place Lanes in Windham, New Hampshire. (Both, photograph by author.)

The first candlepin balls were made of wood. By the early 1900s, however, hard rubber balls hit the scene. Rubber balls, like the Brunswick Mineralite model shown here, dominated the game into the 1970s, when manufacturers started using resins, nylon, polyester, and other synthetic materials. (Courtesy of ICBA.)

Candlepins have come a long way from Pop White's wooden dowels, but one thing did not change. Candlepins were made of wood for decades. Wooden pins splintered and split from the constant ball action, and manufacturers tried different ways to extend pin life, including end caps and a plastic coating over a wooden core. Nothing changed, however, until the Garland Manufacturing Company tried something new. (Photograph by author.)

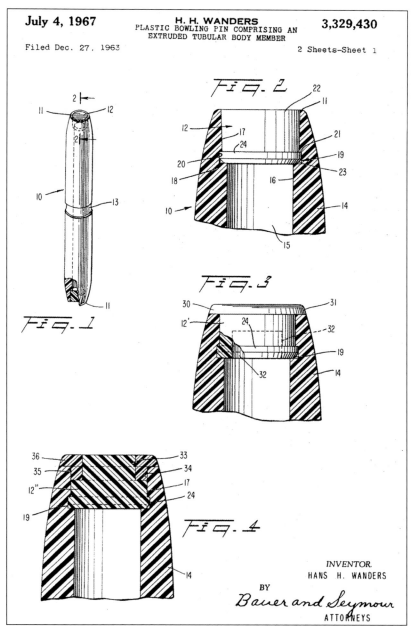

July 4, 1967   **H. H. WANDERS**   3,329,430
PLASTIC BOWLING PIN COMPRISING AN
EXTRUDED TUBULAR BODY MEMBER

Filed Dec. 27, 1963   2 Sheets—Sheet 1

Fig. 1

Fig. 2

Fig. 3

Fig. 4

INVENTOR.
HANS H. WANDERS
BY
Bauer and Seymour
ATTORNEYS

The Garland Manufacturing Company got its start in 1866 by making loom pickers for the textile industry from durable water buffalo hides. The family-owned business began experimenting with plastic resin in the 1950s. Past president Charles Garland recalls how his father tested formulations in the oven in the family's kitchen. At the suggestion of Chris Anton, of the nearby Big 20 Bowling Center, Garland made some plastic candlepins. Anton asked bowlers at his center to test the prototypes, which were then yellow instead of the familiar white. The new pins were expected to last 8–10 years, a significant advantage over the short-lived wooden versions, and plastic pins (now white) became the industry standard. Shown here is a detail from Garland's patent application. (Courtesy of US Patent and Trademark Office.)

Three

NAMES IN THE GAME
PEOPLE AND PLACES

During the heyday of candlepin bowling, nearly every city or town had at least one candlepin alley. Today, about 100 candlepin houses remain in New England. Most of the region's candlepin centers are independently owned, many are family affairs, and a few are in private clubs or social organizations. Here are the stories behind some of the people and places in the game.

The Wal-Lex Recreation Center was a family affair from the start. Brothers-in-law Frederick Tortola, John Rando, and George Rando opened 20 candlepin lanes in 1947 on an apple orchard in Waltham, Massachusetts. "Business boomed right from the start, especially with bowlers from the Waltham Watch Factory," Tortola told the *Boston Globe* in 1997. "We didn't have enough lanes for them. Women eventually started bowling, too, and started their own leagues. We were buried." Over the years, the facility expanded to offer 60 lanes of bowling, roller skating, billiards, miniature golf, and video games. Wal-Lex closed in 2002. The recreation center needed too many repairs, and the second-generation owners Fred Tortola Jr. and his brother-in-law Peter Collura could not afford to make the required investments. (Both, courtesy of Waltham Historical Society.)

WAL-LEX SUMMER FUN SPECIAL

☐ **BOWLING — 2 Strings**   Daily 9:00 A.M. - 5:00 P.M. and Tues. Nite
NO SUBSTITUTION

☐ **ROLLERSKATING — 2 Hours**   Daily and Tues. Nite Inquire for Skating Hours
NO SUBSTITUTION

☐ **GOLF — 1 Round**   Daily 9:00 A.M. - 5:00 P.M. and Tues. Nite
NO SUBSTITUTION

This Ticket Good Only July and August,
Monday through Friday 9:00 A.M.-5:00 P.M.
and Tues. Nites

Ernie Sawyer Jr. and his father opened Sawyer's Bowladrome in Northborough, Massachusetts, in 1953. They had acquired the building a few years earlier; it housed a few pool tables and not much more. When they decided to add bowling, they excavated a basement crawl space, using shovels and wheelbarrows, to make room for six candlepin lanes. (Photograph by author.)

The Sawyers imported the wooden lanes from an alley in Clinton, Massachusetts, and invested in automatic pinsetters a few years later. The pool tables eventually gave way to a space for family-friendly events. An accomplished candlepinner himself, Sawyer quickly dismissed tenpin bowling because it is too easy. "Anyone can bowl a perfect game with enough practice," he said about the big-ball game. (Photograph by author.)

Fred Smith opened a billiards hall in Springfield, Massachusetts, in 1902, and the business is still open today. After moving to the current location on Worthington Street in 1914, Smith added 22 lanes of candlepin bowling on three upper floors. When business dropped in the 1960s, the lanes were dismantled and installed in a Connecticut bowling alley. (Photograph by author.)

Bowl-O-Mat opened in Beverly, Massachusetts, in 1954. Ted Christopher, whose father and uncle owned the center, started bowling at age five and eventually took over the family business with a cousin. "I've been there my whole life," he told the *Boston Globe* when he retired in 2017. Bowl-O-Mat was shuttered after Christopher's retirement, and the contents were auctioned off. (Photograph by author.)

Mike Walker wanted to own a bowling center since he was five years old. Now in his early 30s, he is the sole owner and operator of the Big 20 Bowling Center in Scarborough, Maine. The 20-lane venue was first called State O' Maine when it opened in 1950—the sign is still standing—but the Big 20 name soon stuck. (Photograph by author.)

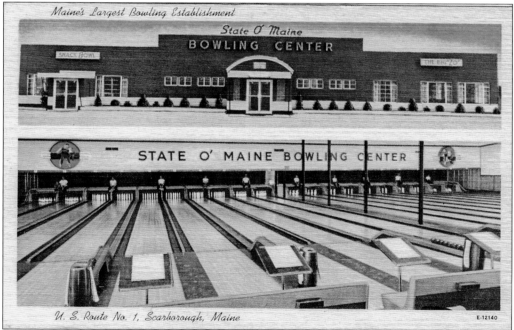

Sofokli Anton, known as Mike, was the original owner. His son Chris, who was a champion bowler, took over the business from his father and ran the house for about 30 years. An early postcard shows the days when duckpin, tenpin, and candlepin bowling were all available, and pin boys were ready for action. Today, Big 20 is an all-candlepin center. (Author's collection.)

Putnam Street Lanes is the oldest surviving candlepin alley in New England. Opened around the turn of the 20th century, the second-story house is on a side street in downtown Fitchburg, Massachusetts. Gary Therrien is the current owner, and his father and uncle owned the 10-lane house before him. (Photograph by author.)

An arrow on Bridge Street in Shelburne Falls, Massachusetts, reads "Bowling" and directs people through a narrow alley. On the other side, they will find Shelburne Falls Bowling Alley. Opened in 1906, the eight-lane house is the second-oldest bowling alley in New England. "In 1906 they came down the alley and bowled here, and they're still doing it today," owner Joanne Gaulin told *Yankee Magazine*. "We love that." (Photograph by author.)

In the days before air-conditioning, well-heeled Bostonians left the city each summer in search of cool breezes and shady spots. Summer folk mostly stayed in guesthouses, which boasted amenities like upright pianos, tennis, croquet, and farm-fresh meals. Some also had bowling alleys on-site. In 2016, the New Boston Historical Society documented the New Hampshire town's last candlepin alley shortly before it was demolished, shown here. The single lane was in the hayloft of a barn on the grounds of Prospect Cottage, a guesthouse owned by Florence Adelaide Dodge Atwood. The alley was maple, the pins were wooden, and the balls had finger holes. Grain sacks were used as bumpers. Locals used the lane well into the 1960s, often signing their names on one of the walls; signatures date from 1926 to 1967. (Both, photograph by Dan Rothman; courtesy of New Boston Historical Society.)

Needham Bowlaway is the oldest candlepin house in metropolitan Boston. Opened in 1917, the alley has eight lanes in a basement in suburban Needham, Massachusetts. The ball returns were made by Brunswick, the pinsetting machines date from Bowl-Mor's first production run, and some of the lanes were reclaimed from Wal-Lex in Waltham. (Photograph by author.)

Ray and Edgar Simoneau opened Leda Lanes in Nashua, New Hampshire, in 1959. "Everyone said they would never make it out there in the boonies," Ed Simoneau's daughter Louise Patterson said in 1989. But Leda Lanes thrived, doubling in size from 18 lanes to 36 and adding billiard tables, video games, a lounge called Kegler's Den, and an annex with glow bowling. (Photograph by author.)

Salvatore Gangi Sr. transformed a garage into the Woburn Bowladrome in a suburb north of Boston in 1940. It was not easy; a rock formation known as Nanny Goat Hill stood in his way. But after "hundreds of blasting operations," as a publication celebrating the bowling alley's 50th anniversary described the effort, construction moved forward. Some 80 years later, the Gangi family still runs the place. (Photograph by author.)

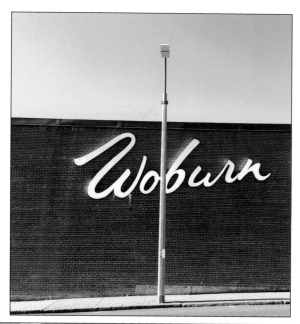

Walking into Wakefield Bowladrome transports bowlers back to the 1950s. The mid-century typography, the jaunty gentleman and stylish lady gracing the signs above the restroom doors, the glass-block entry, and the streamlined ball returns all contribute to a classic candlepin experience. Sal Orifice purchased the former Sunlight Alleys in Wakefield, Massachusetts, in 1952. He rebuilt the place from scratch after a devastating fire in 1959. (Photograph by author.)

Owen Martin's father, Russell, built the Bowl-A-Rama in the heart of Sanford, Maine, in 1959. "People bowled three or four times a week," Martin recalled. "They bowled in leagues, and then they bowled on the weekends. The place would be open until midnight." (Photograph by Elizabeth Budington.)

Capitalizing on the bowling boom, a group of local businessmen built All-Star Lanes on the outskirts of town in 1968, and the two spots competed for the next 20 years. Owen Martin took over Bowl-A-Rama from his dad in the late 1970s, after a stint as a merchant marine. In 1988, Martin bought All-Star Lanes and renamed it Bowl-A-Rama. The building housing Martin's original bowling alley was replaced with a park. (Photograph by author.)

King Bowling Lanes opened to great fanfare in November 1939. The 10-lane center in Goffstown, New Hampshire, was built at a cost of $30,000, and a newspaper advertisement for opening night touted the first-floor location, air-conditioning, and parking. The LaRochelle family purchased the bowling center from the Gagnon family in 1954 and has owned it ever since. Note the foot pedals used to reset the pins. (Photograph by author.)

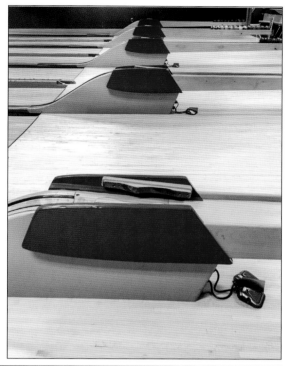

The Kenmore Bowladrome was located next to Fenway Park, home of the Boston Red Sox, for almost 50 years. The basement-level alley had 20 candlepin lanes. When the bowladrome closed in 2004, the Red Sox repurposed some of the lanes into bar tops for an event venue in the right-field roof deck. (Photograph by Tom Marchessault.)

This is a story of two bowling families. Bill Genimatas built the Bowl-O-Rama on US Route 1 in Portsmouth, New Hampshire, in 1956. His children Nick and Kathleen worked alongside their father for years and eventually took over. By 2018, they were ready to retire. Bart Maderios ran the youth programs at Pilgrim Lanes in Haverhill, Massachusetts, with help from his teenage son Andrew. Father and son talked about owning a bowling center for years but never found

the right opportunity. Instead, Andrew worked at Bowl-O-Rama while pursuing his education, eventually taking a teaching job in Maine, and Bart kept his day job. But they stayed in touch with the Genimatases, and when the family was ready to sell Bowl-O-Rama, Andrew and his parents bought the center. (Photograph by author.)

Bob Lawton borrowed $750 to open an arcade and miniature golf course at Weirs Beach in 1952. Twelve years later, he moved the Weirs Sports Center to Meredith, New Hampshire, and renamed it Funspot. The entertainment center expanded to include miniature golf, theme parks, arcade games, and bingo. Some arcade tickets are shown here. The complex added 10 lanes of candlepin and 10 lanes of tenpin bowling in 1988. (Photograph by author.)

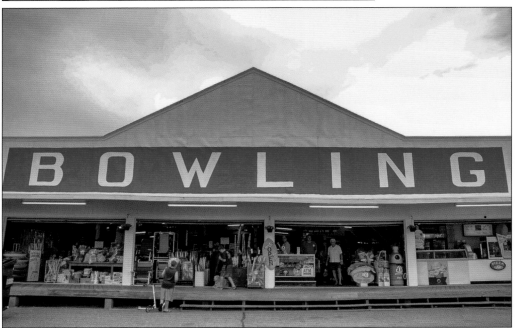

Bowling in York Beach, Maine, is a beachy affair. A painted sign simply reads "Bowling," and the alleys are adjacent to the Fun-O-Rama arcade on Short Sands Beach. No bowling shoes are required at this casual spot. Customers are encouraged to bowl in their street shoes—or sandals—and the sand crunches underfoot. (Photograph by Kevin Hong.)

Mark and Melissa Ricci are both champion bowlers. "There are very few couples that are both elite in their own right and can actually bowl together," Mark observed. In 2007, Melissa took home the $5,000 prize for 20 strings at Leda Lanes in Nashua, New Hampshire. She scored 2,450 and set a house single record of 191. Four years later, Mark notched a record high score of 519 for three strings at Metro Bowl in Peabody, Massachusetts. But it all evens out in the end. "She has the biggest trophy in the house," Mark said. "But I have more world records." (Photograph by Kevin Hong.)

The Riccis took over Riverwalk Lanes in Amesbury, Massachusetts, in 2012. The eight-lane candlepin house opened in 1946 and was previously known as Lafayette Lanes. The ball returns still have the original Brunswick tags. (Photograph by author.)

Lou Pasquale has done pretty much everything at Boston Bowl except one. He does not bowl. "I take that back," he said upon further reflection. "I threw a ball to check a machine that was broken." His lack of bowling notwithstanding, Pasquale was the go-to guy for decades at this bowling center in the city's Dorchester neighborhood. (Photograph by author.)

Boston Bowl opened in 1960 as a tenpin house—the candlepins came later—and Pasquale was there from the start. "I was here night and day," he recalled. "I slept behind the machines." When the mechanic called in sick, Pasquale learned to fix the pinsetters himself. Eventually, he became the manager. Now in his 90s, he no longer works every day, but he retains the title of vice president of community relations. (Photograph by Elizabeth Budington.)

A large dog greets visitors to Brian's Bowlaway in Gardner, Massachusetts. Brian Favreau bought the place in 1989, but the center dates from the 1930s. The wooden ball returns are painted to match the pastel Brunswick masking units at the end of each lane, shown here, and scoring is with paper and pencil. (Photograph by author.)

Asked about the appeal of candlepin, Favreau said, "It's the challenge of it. Anything can happen." Gardner is home to two bowling centers—Brian's Bowlaway and Gardner Ten Pins. Each displays a sign in the shape of a bowling pin, but that is where the similarities end. Players are loyal to their chosen sport, and there is not much crossover. "It's in their blood," Favreau said about candlepin players. (Photograph by author.)

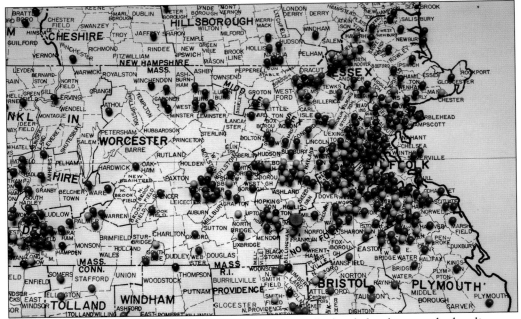

The Parrella family has been in the bowling business for three generations. Emilio Parrella emigrated from Italy in 1926 and worked at a rubber factory in Newton, Massachusetts, in the 1940s. He developed a process to repair and refinish bowling balls—which were often nicked by the pinsetting equipment—and founded E. Parrella Co., Inc., known as EPCO, in 1952. In 1960, EPCO began to manufacture balls for all types of small-ball bowling, including candlepins, duckpins, and five pins. Today, Emilio's sons Robert, Richard, and John Parrella run the Massachusetts-based company, along with its distribution affiliate Paramount Industries. Robert and his son Scott own Park Place Lanes (shown here) in Windham, New Hampshire, where Scott is the manager. The map, at Paramount's headquarters, marks bowling centers of all types across New England. (Both, photograph by author.)

Ralph Semb set the single-game record in 1984 when he rolled a 245 at Community Lanes in Westfield, Massachusetts. "Seven strikes in a row and three spares," he recalls. Rushing to the event, he forgot his bowling balls and shoes and accomplished the feat using rental shoes and house balls. Semb was already the owner of French King Bowling Center in Erving, Massachusetts, shown here, which he built with his father in 1959. (Photograph by author.)

Despite his record-setting string, Semb lost the tournament and walked away with just $50 in prize money. Winner Charlie Jutras received $275. The high score has been tied once, by Chris Sargent in 2011, but Semb's record of seven consecutive strikes still stands. After Community Lanes closed, the plaque commemorating Semb's record was moved to Canal Lanes in Southampton, Massachusetts. (Photograph by Bill Ballou.)

Not all candlepin lanes are open to the public. They can be found in country clubs, social organizations, church basements, and hotels. This photograph shows candlepin bowling during World War II at the Franklin Square House, a residential hotel for single working women in Boston, Massachusetts. (Courtesy of the Boston Public Library, Leslie Jones Collection.)

In Waltham, Massachusetts, the city's recreation department built four candlepin lanes in the basement of an old school building that now houses city offices. The lanes and equipment were installed in 2014, and Waltham offers bowling programs for seniors, preschoolers, and family groups. (Photograph by author.)

No one remembers exactly why or when candlepins came to Wyoming, Ohio, but a plaque on the wall celebrates the achievements of Smith Allen Coffing, who set a high single and triple in 1922. The six lanes were installed in the basement of the Wyoming Civic Center in 1948 after the previous Amusement Hall burned to the ground. (Courtesy of Wyoming Historical Society.)

Turnpike Bowladrome opened in Cambridge, Massachusetts, in 1942. Brothers John and Tony Martignetti bought the property in 1983 and renamed it Lanes and Games, shown here. The two-story center offered candlepins downstairs and tenpins upstairs. The brothers retired in 2017 and sold the property for residential development. When the lanes closed, one bowler summed up what many were feeling. "It's a real Cambridge institution," he told WBUR's Sharon Brody. (Photograph by Sharon Brody; courtesy of WBUR.)

Sometimes it is all about the signs. Candlepin houses often installed distinctive signs to mark the spot. Neon signs were still going strong in the 1950s, but plastic signs began to appear by the end of the decade. Two Massachusetts bowling centers about 10 years and 10 miles apart show this transition. Sunnyside Bowladrome, which opened in Danvers in 1950, has a roof-mounted neon sign typical of the era, complete with flashing arrow. Wakefield Bowladrome, opened in 1959, welcomes players with a freestanding plastic sign. (Both, photograph by author.)

Signs offer a clue to the past at some candlepin houses. The Big 20 Bowling Center in Scarborough, Maine, was once called State O' Maine. The name was changed early on, and a new freestanding sign beckons travelers on US Route 1, but the original roof-mounted sign still stands. (Photograph by Elizabeth Budington.)

For Lanes and Games in Cambridge, Massachusetts, the carpet told the tale. The former Turnpike Bowladrome was rebranded when the Martignetti brothers purchased the venue in the 1980s. The signs were changed, but the carpeted walls in the candlepin lanes read "Turnpike" until the center closed in 2017. (Photograph by Sharon Brody; courtesy of WBUR.)

Colonial Bowling Center is the last candlepin house standing in Worcester, Massachusetts, where it all began. Now in his 90s, Nick Andreson opened the spot in 1960. Shown here in a photograph from the opening celebration are, from left to right, Nick's brother James Andreson, Nick's wife Anastasia Andreson, and two unidentified men. (Courtesy of WHM.)

Colonial has barely changed since opening night and, until recently, still had a rotary-dial telephone. Now treasured for its mid-century charm, Colonial was once part of the new wave of modern suburban centers. For years, candlepin alleys typically squeezed six or eight lanes into downtown buildings. But like many centers built in the 1950s and 1960s, Colonial is a freestanding structure that offered conveniences like air-conditioning and a parking lot. (Photograph by Kevin Hong.)

On New Year's Day in 1950, Central Park Lanes, shown here, opened in East Boston, Massachusetts. Chuck Vozzella joined the family business straight out of high school and runs the place today. A professional bowler, Vozzella captured the 1989 Massachusetts state doubles championship with partner Joe Stella. But before that, Vozzella was a high school baseball star and was inducted into the Peabody High School Athletic Hall of Fame in 2016. "I think my bowling helped my pitching in baseball in terms of accuracy," he told the *East Boston Times-Free Press*. "Pitching on the mound and throwing strikes and throwing at the head pin in bowling are a lot alike." (Both, photograph by author.)

On the morning of September 22, 1980, four bodies were discovered in a back room of Sammy White's Brighton Bowl in Boston, Massachusetts. Former Red Sox catcher Sammy White owned the bowling center, which was the filming location for Channel 5's *Candlepin Bowling* for years. The victims were George Hagelstein, Donald Doroni, David Cobe, and Brian Cobe. All were employees of the bowling center; each had been bludgeoned with a bowling pin and shot once in the head. The safe was open, and $4,800 was missing. Former employee Brian A. Dyer was arrested about a week later and convicted at trial. He was sentenced to four consecutive life terms and died in prison in 2011. Sammy White's closed in 1986. (Both, courtesy of the Suffolk County District Attorney's Office.)

Four

OUTSIDE THE LANES

CANDLEPINS ON
TELEVISION AND BEYOND

Starting in 1958, television took candlepin bowling outside the lanes and into living rooms across New England. *Candlepin Bowling* was the first show and the longest-running. About 200,000 households tuned in weekly, and those ratings sometimes eclipsed those of Boston's professional sports teams. The televised competitions served as free advertising for the game, and viewers flocked to bowling centers eager to try candlepin bowling for themselves.

For nearly four decades, Boston-area viewers were glued to their television sets on Saturday afternoons. *Candlepin Bowling* aired from 1958 to 1996, mostly on WCVB-TV Channel 5. Jim Britt was the inaugural host. Don Gillis, pictured here, took over in 1961 and stayed for the next 35 years. (Courtesy of WCVB.)

Two players faced off against each other in a three-string contest for prize money, merchandise, and a trophy. Winners returned each week until an opponent scored more pins and took over the top spot. From 1976 to 1995, championship shows were broadcast live at the end of each season. The show was taped at three now-shuttered candlepin houses in the Boston metropolitan area: Boylston Bowladrome, Sammy White's Brighton Bowl, and Fairway Sports World (proprietor Helen Sellew is pictured here). (Courtesy of ICBA.)

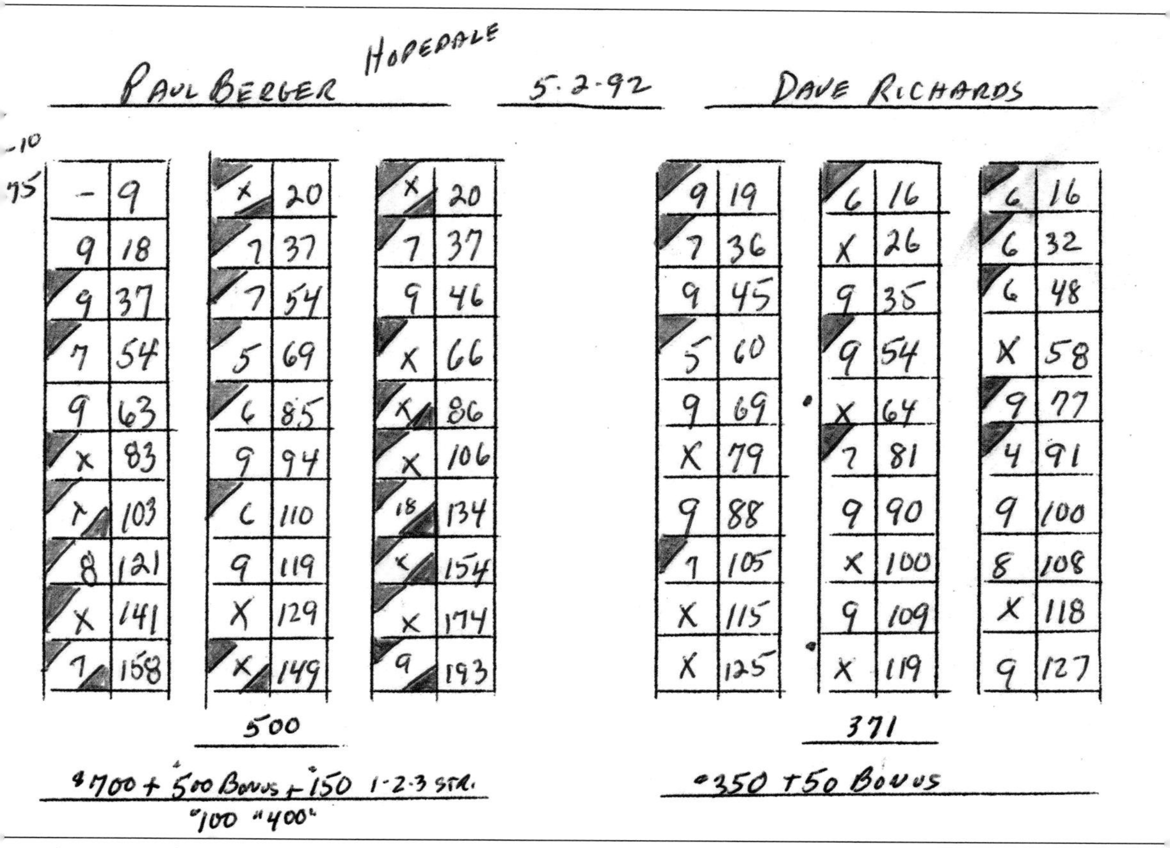

PAUL BERGER HOPEDALE 5-2-92 **DAVE RICHARDS**

Paul Berger — 500

String 1		String 2		String 3	
–	9	X	20	X	20
9	18	7	37	7	37
9	37	7	54	9	46
7	54	5	69	X	66
9	63	6	85	X	86
X	83	9	94	X	106
7	103	C	110	18	134
8	121	9	119	X	154
X	141	X	129	X	174
7	158	X	149	9	193

500

$700 + 500 Bonus + 150 1-2-3 str.
"100 "400"

Dave Richards — 371

String 1		String 2		String 3	
9	19	6	16	6	16
7	36	X	26	6	32
9	45	9	35	6	48
5	60	9	54	X	58
9	69	X	64	9	77
X	79	7	81	4	91
9	88	9	90	9	100
7	105	X	100	8	108
X	115	9	109	X	118
X	125	X	119	9	127

371

$350 + 50 Bonus

"Average, ordinary people became superstars because of this quirky game," said Mike Morin about televised bowling. Morin is a retired candlepin broadcaster who discovered the game when he moved to New England in the 1980s. His book *Lunch with Tommy and Stasia* tells the story of these unlikely celebrities. The title refers to two of the best-known players in the game: Tom Olszta and Stasia Czernicki. "The two of them—because of TV, and only because of TV—became celebrities as big as Larry Bird or Bobby Orr," Morin said. Among many other stories, Morin's book recounts the historic 1992 match between Paul Berger and Dave Richards. Berger scored 500 pins over three strings and set the record for highest triple on *Candlepin Bowling*. The scoresheet is shown here. (Courtesy of Frank DeLuca.)

Tom Olszta won the Massachusetts Bowling Association state singles title in 1973 when he was just 16. He eventually appeared on television bowling shows over 200 times, including a 22-week run on *Candlepin Bowling*. Channel 5 candlepin hosts Ed Harding (left) and Don Gillis (center) appeared with Olszta here. (Courtesy of ICBA.)

Stasia Czernicki is considered the best woman bowler in the history of candlepin. She was a world champion eight times and a Massachusetts state champion 12 times. She logged 55 appearances on Channel 5. Here, Czernicki (center) holds her trophy for women's world champion in 1970 with Joe Sacco (left) and Silvio Angelotti. (Photograph by Roger's Studio; courtesy of ICBA.)

Candlepin Bowling was the longest-running candlepin show on television, but it had plenty of company. Other shows included *Candlepins for Cash, Candlepin Stars and Strikes, Big Shot Bowling,* and *Candlepin Challenge.* Brian Leary hosted two shows on WCVB-TV in the 1980s: *Candlepin Superbowl* and *Candlepin Doubles.* Here, he is pictured at left with champion bowler Joe Tavernese in 1989. (Courtesy of Brian Leary.)

Candlepin Stars and Strikes aired on WNDS-TV from 1983 to 2005. The show was taped at Park Place Lanes in Windham, New Hampshire, through 1997 and then at Leda Lanes in Nashua, New Hampshire. In 2005, hosts Mike Morin (left) and Dick Lutsk were raising funds for junior bowling programs at Pilgrim Lanes in Haverhill, Massachusetts. (Photograph by Kevin Cormier; courtesy of Mike Morin.)

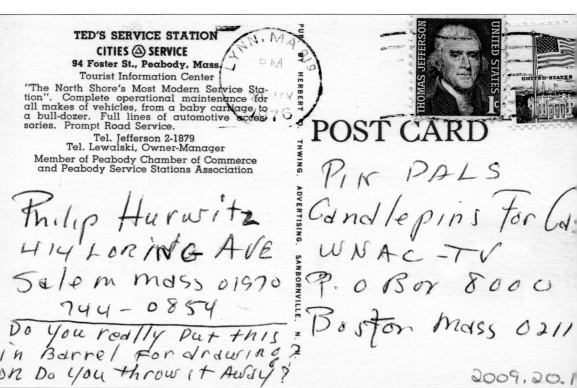

TED'S SERVICE STATION
CITIES ⓐ SERVICE
94 Foster St., Peabody, Mass.
Tourist Information Center

"The North Shore's Most Modern Service Station". Complete operational maintenance for all makes of vehicles, from a baby carriage to a bull-dozer. Full lines of automotive accessories. Prompt Road Service.
Tel. Jefferson 2-1879
Tel. Lewalski, Owner-Manager
Member of Peabody Chamber of Commerce and Peabody Service Stations Association

POST CARD

Philip Hurwitz
414 Loring Ave
Salem mass 01970
744 - 0854
Do you really put this in Barrel for drawing? or Do you throw it Away?

Pin Pals
Candlepins for Ca.
WNAC - TV
P. o Box 8000
Boston mass 0211

2009.20.1

Paul Wambach, manager of Colonial Bowling Center in Worcester, Massachusetts, recalled calling his mother, Pauline, herself a competitive bowler, when *Candlepin Bowling* was canceled in 1996. "I said, 'Ma, I've got some bad news.' She said, 'Who died?' I said, 'Ma, it's worse. The *Candlepin Bowling* show is going off the air.' And there was a little bit of a pause, and she said, 'Well, fine. Why don't they just take off *Wheel of Fortune*, too. I'll get rid of my TV altogether.' That was it for her. *Candlepin Bowling* and *Wheel of Fortune*." For John Tobin, the must-see show was *Candlepins for Cash*. The former Boston city councilor recalled watching every night with his dad. "We used to laugh and giggle at *Candlepins for Cash* because it was regular people," he said. The Pin Pals were part of the appeal. These were viewers who submitted postcards—sometimes with snarky comments—in hopes of being selected to win prizes along with the bowler. (Courtesy of the Peabody Institute Library.)

"Our subject is love because our subject is bowling. Candlepin bowling." So wrote Elizabeth McCracken in *Bowlaway*. The multigenerational novel centers around Bertha Truitt and the candlepin alley she built in the fictional town of Salford, Massachusetts. McCracken grew up in the Boston area, and her affection for candlepin bowling infuses her book. "I like the fact that perfection is unattainable," she said. (Photograph by Edward Carey.)

THE GAME OF
Candlepin Bowling

By FLORENCE E. GREENLEAF
As told to Paul C. Tedford
CARL E. GREENE, Historian

In 1985, Florence E. Greenleaf published *The Game of Candlepin Bowling* in collaboration with Carl E. Greene and Paul C. Telford. Greenleaf taught physical education in Springfield, Massachusetts, and wrote her master's thesis about candlepin bowling. "Our book deals with The Game of Candlepins," the book began. "It is the most prevalent of all small-ball games and universally recognized as the most scientific of all forms of bowling." (Author's collection.)

After retiring from the *Worcester Telegram & Gazette*, sportswriter Bill Ballou started a new adventure. Bowling the Commonwealth was his quest to roll at every candlepin house in Massachusetts—commercial and private. He described some of the highlights of the tour in the *Telegram*: "I had to set my own pins in Lynn, was skunked by stringers in Adams, disturbed a memorial service in Ipswich, and bowled for the first time in more than 50 years at Denis LaTour's restored alleys in the Pythian Building in Whitinsville." Throughout, he got to meet new people, reconnect with old friends, and just have fun. Pictured here are the lanes at the Boys and Girls Club of Lynn (above), which required players to set their own pins, and the Turner Hill Country Club in Ipswich (below), where he encountered that wake. (Both, photograph by Bill Ballou.)

Boston Red Sox Hall of Famer Jim Rice is known to be an avid candlepin bowler. In 1981, he filmed a commercial to promote the game for the Massachusetts Bowling Association. The shoot took place at Turnpike Bowladrome in Cambridge, Massachusetts, which later became Lanes and Games before closing in 2017. But the story does not end there. In *Lunch with Tommy and Stasia*, Tom Olszta revealed that he was the ghost bowler for the commercial. "Jim Rice did a commercial, and I did all the bowling for it," he recalled. "They just had shots of him on the approach throwing the ball. I did the bowling for the whole commercial." (Both, photograph by Sharon Brody; courtesy of WBUR.)

Leslie Jones was a photographer for the *Boston Herald-Traveler* newspaper from 1917 to 1956. He photographed Will Rogers, William Jennings Bryan, Billy Sunday, Aimee Semple McPherson, Mary Pickford, Clara Bow, and other public figures of the day. But much of his work documented the everyday lives of people in the Boston metropolitan area. In a photograph from around 1954, Jones captured three unidentified women bowling for the camera, complete with hose and heels (above). That same year, he photographed an unidentified man choosing a candlepin ball. (Both, courtesy of the Boston Public Library, Leslie Jones Collection.)

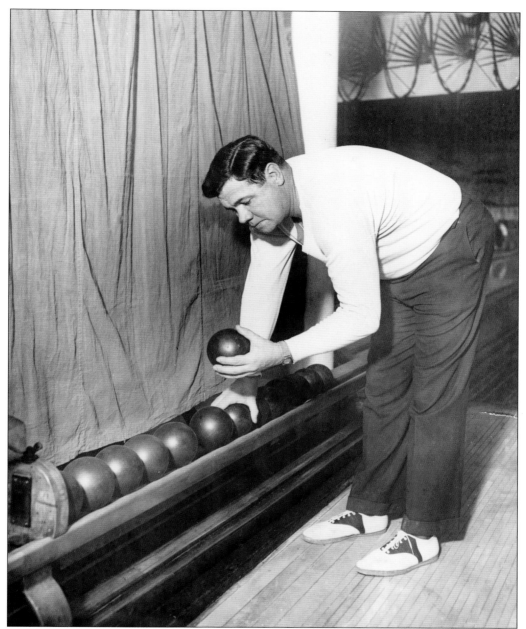

Was Babe Ruth a connoisseur of candlepin or was he a duckpin man? He was often photographed at small-ball houses, but the pins were never visible. Advocates of each game have claimed Ruth as a player, but the answer is always just out of reach. Could geography offer a clue? Ruth lived in Massachusetts for years, but he was born in Baltimore, where duckpins were said to originate. This 1930 photograph was captioned candlepin, but it does not say where. He was already a New Yorker by then, where neither game prevailed. So, did Babe Ruth roll candles or ducks? The mystery remains. (Courtesy of the National Baseball Hall of Fame and Museum.)

Bowling movies like *The Big Lebowski* featured tenpins, but candlepin bowling has turned up in a few Boston-centric works. The 1999 film *Southie* included a scene at South Boston Candlepin (shown here), and the old-school house also turned up on *Anthony Bourdain: No Reservations*. After rolling a few strings, Bourdain described his experience as an "all too brief run of luck followed by a crushing and shameful defeat of the worst kind." A 1992 *Saturday Night Live* sketch featuring Glenn Close—herself a candlepin bowler—parodied New Englanders and their love of the game. Finally, candlepin bowling played a key role in an episode of *The Simpsons* where Homer visited fictional houses like Bulger's Bowl-O-Rama and the Lanes of Eddie Coyle. (Both, photograph by author.)

As a way to give back to the community, Brighton Bowl invites local students of all ages for pizza and bowling. "Some kids have never been in a restaurant; most kids have never bowled," said owner Tom Keane. "And it's really incredible to watch." (Photograph by author.)

When former Boston Red Sox pitcher Manny Delcarmen and business partner Jose Diaz established the Boston Athletic Academy, they held a fundraiser at Ron's Gourmet Ice Cream and Bowling in Hyde Park, Massachusetts. "Growing up in Hyde Park, we would spend hours and hours at Ron's when baseball wasn't in season, staying off of the streets, trying to out-bowl one another for bragging rights," Diaz said in a 2018 newspaper interview. (Photograph by author.)

As a young soldier in World War II, Lou Pasquale suffered a grievous injury. Lying in a field for 14 hours, he had a heavenly vision and promised to help an individual every day of his life if he returned home. When he came to work at Boston Bowl in 1960, he kept that promise. During his years at the bowling center, Pasquale reached out to at-risk youth, counseled patrons, and worked with community organizations. Boston mayor Martin Walsh honored Pasquale for his community service in 2019 by renaming the intersection outside the bowling center as Lou Pasquale Square. (Photograph by author.)

In 1996, the Commonwealth of Massachusetts paid a similar tribute to a candlepin legend. A section of Thompson Road in the town of Webster was renamed Stasia Czernicki Memorial Way to honor the town's native daughter. (Photograph by author.)

Five

STAYING IN THE GAME
CANDLEPIN LOOKS TO THE FUTURE

Candlepin bowling operators are looking for new ways to keep the 19th-century sport relevant. Many proprietors are focusing on the next generation of bowlers with family-friendly features to encourage youngsters to get involved in the game. Others have introduced menus with upscale items like flatbread pizza, craft beer, and specialty ice cream. Finally, some players have taken the game online, and one fan even wants to revive a famous television show.

Julius Covitz started Twentieth Century Bowling Alleys in the Hyde Park neighborhood of Boston, Massachusetts, in the 1950s. His son Ron joined the family business in the late 1960s and introduced his award-winning ice cream. Today, Ron's son Jay Covitz runs the combination ice-cream parlor and bowling alley, now called Ron's Gourmet Ice Cream and Bowling. (Photograph by author.)

Birthdays and bowling are part of growing up in New England, and most bowling centers host children's birthday parties. Depending on the size of the venue, the party might include food, cake, a customized playlist, party favors, and—of course—bowling. Here, Ron's gets ready for its next birthday celebration. (Photograph by author.)

Cosmic bowling hit the scene in the 1990s. Trying to redefine bowling for a new generation, candlepin operators created disco-inspired light and sound shows on the lanes. Often reserved for weekends, cosmic bowling uses laser lights to wash the lanes with colors and patterns. Black lights make everything glow, and music is always playing. Here are the lights at Needham Bowlaway in Needham, Massachusetts. (Photograph by author.)

To make the game easier for children and beginners—or at least less frustrating—many candlepin proprietors introduced bumpers in the 1990s. These barriers take many forms, but they are designed to direct errant throws back into the lane and to keep balls out of the gutter. A young Nate calculates his next move at Lanes and Games in Cambridge, Massachusetts, about 1993. (Courtesy of Janet and Tom Cohan.)

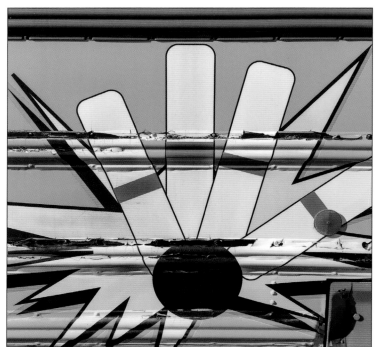

Owen Martin uses his charter bus business to support a new generation of bowlers. The owner of Bowl-A-Rama in Sanford, Maine, wanted to make it easier for children to bowl. So, he introduced the "Let's Go Bowling" bus. Martin drives the brightly decorated vehicle (detail shown here) to pick up students at the end of the school day and bring them to the lanes for an after-school league. (Photograph by author.)

Zach Sundberg, who owns Needham Bowlaway, shown here, loves that candlepin bowling is an activity for the whole family. "You can bring three generations, and everybody is going to have fun together," he said. Sundberg developed a semiautomatic scoring system to keep young players engaged. "When the kids are involved in the process, they learn how to bowl and they learn how to keep score," he said. (Photograph by author.)

When Andrew Maderios took over Bowl-O-Rama in Portsmouth, New Hampshire, he replaced the plastic chairs with cushy loveseats, added a state-of-the-art scoring system, updated the arcade, and opened a restaurant. He believes that changes like this, many of which have been introduced by younger proprietors like himself, are critical to the future of the game. "The more minds that we put together, the more ideas that we can share, the stronger the game will become," he said. "There are a lot of young people in the game now, and I think that it has done nothing but help." (Both, photograph by author.)

A neon sign marks the spot for Cape Ann Lanes, which dates from 1959 in Gloucester, Massachusetts. Caitlin and Nic Pszenny held their wedding reception there in 2016, and by the end of the year, Nic and his uncle Jim Frontiero owned the place. Aside from weddings, Cape Ann Lanes hosts children's birthday parties, live music, and fundraisers. A brewpub is in the works. "We see our

bowling center as a community hub," said Caitlin, who is the general manager. "We want to make it a welcoming place for everyone." As part of its commitment to working with the bowlers of tomorrow, Cape Ann Lanes has hosted qualifying rounds for *Candlepin New Generation*, a long-running YouTube competition for players aged 18 and under. (Photograph by author.)

Joseph B. Sacco Sr. and his son Ralph opened Bowl Haven, a bowling alley and billiards hall in Somerville, Massachusetts, in 1939. The house stayed in the family until 2010 when Joseph's grandsons sold Bowl Haven to the Flatbread Company. The historic lanes have retained their vintage look and feel, down to the paper-and-pencil scoring, but now customers can enjoy pizza and drinks while they bowl. (Photograph by author.)

Opened in 1940, the Bowling Bowl was a fixture in Brunswick, Maine. When the alley closed in 2018, US senator Angus King (I-Maine) was among those voicing their concern. But happily for King and his constituents, Brunswick restaurateurs Joe O'Neil and Michael Jerome stepped in to renovate the Bowling Bowl. Now called Bolo's Kitchen, Cantina, and Candlepin, the place combines old-school bowling with a modern Tex-Mex menu. (Photograph by author.)

Beer and bowling are a time-honored tradition, but drinking in the lanes was outlawed in Massachusetts starting in 1962. Bowling alleys with bars could serve alcohol, but customers could not enjoy their beverages while playing. In 2000, the legislature repealed the ruling, and bowlers once again had the right to drink and roll. The exterior walls at Leo's Metro Bowl in Peabody, Massachusetts, display vintage-style beer advertisements. (Photograph by author.)

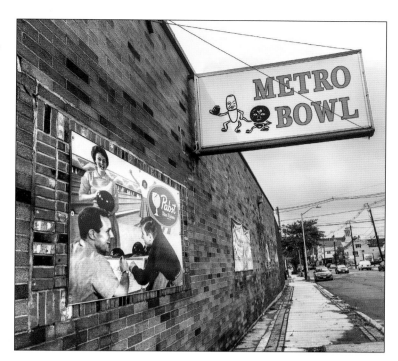

In 2015, Castle Island Brewing Company opened its doors with a line of locally inspired beers. One was named Candlepin. "When we decided to brew an American pale ale that was all about recreation and fun, we knew we had to name it after the New England classic pastime," said president Adam Romanow. "It triggers an emotional, nostalgic response for those who grew up candlepin bowling." (Courtesy of Castle Island Brewing Company.)

Kids Bowl Free lets youngsters bowl two free games a day during the summer at participating bowling centers in the United States and Canada. The program is not limited to candlepin, and over 21 million kids have registered between 2008 and 2019. Besides allowing proprietors to give back to their communities, the program has online tools to support marketing activities. Here, a young man hits the lanes in the pre-Internet era. (Courtesy of WHM.)

Because candlepin bowling is a game of skill, not force, players can roll into their 80s and beyond. Minnie Barden and Blanche Bazata, both from western Massachusetts, made history in 1910 when they bowled in the first public candlepin exhibition between women. Barden, shown here, was still bowling in 1971 when she was inducted into the Candlepin Hall of Fame at the age of 82. (Courtesy of ICBA.)

Brighton Bowl, in Boston, Massachusetts, is a new candlepin alley with a retro flair that serves pizza along with pins. It is a natural combination, said owner Tom Keane. "For family culture, it's a one-stop shop. They can have a good meal, and kids love pizza," he said. "And then the bowling. It all ties in together." (Photograph by author.)

Opened originally in 1958, Park Place Lanes in Windham, New Hampshire, bridges old-school and next-generation bowling. Scott Parrella and his father, Robert, purchased the 36-lane venue in 2015. They installed synthetic surfaces, automatic scoring, and new seating for lanes 1–28 and added a karaoke lounge. But lanes 29–36 still offer a classic experience from the early 1980s, with maple lanes and semiautomatic scorekeeping. (Photograph by author.)

ATLANTIC CANDLEPIN Singles TOUR

The Atlantic Candlepin Singles Tour (ACST) is a travel league started in 2017 by Frank DeLuca and Mike Miccichi. Thirty-two pro bowlers compete in head-to-head matches at candlepin houses, and games are livestreamed on Facebook. (Courtesy of Frank DeLuca.)

Brendan O'Dowd helped form the ACST semipro division to offer a competitive outlet for "those who might leave the sport otherwise." He took a break for about 20 years after *Candlepin Bowling* went off the air and returned to find that the candlepin houses he remembered were gone. "I made it my goal to visit as many candlepin centers as I could before they all had a similar fate," he said. As a travel league, ACST gave O'Dowd an opportunity to make those visits. Shown here is one of his favorite spots, Colonial Bowling Center in Worcester, Massachusetts. (Photograph by author.)

King of the Palace is a tournament at New Palace Lanes in Fitchburg, Massachusetts. Fitchburg Access Television produces the show, which runs on local access channels and on YouTube. Commentators include proprietor Dave Maattala and pro bowler Dennis Nuzzo. (Photograph by Brendan O'Dowd.)

Alley Chat was a candlepin bowling podcast hosted by Frank DeLuca and Kyle Bruce. The production recapped bowling matches and interviewed bowling greats like Dan Murphy, the accomplished bowler, proprietor, instructor, and television host. Murphy was previously part owner of Boutwell's Bowling Center in Concord, New Hampshire, shown here. *Alley Chat* is no longer an active podcast, but its YouTube channel posts classic televised bowling matches. (Photograph by author.)

Will televised candlepin bowling make a comeback? John Tobin hopes so. A Boston-area producer for live comedy shows, Tobin currently owns the rights to the name *Candlepins for Cash* and would like to revive the show. His ideas include everything from a band called the Lucky Strikes to mascots dressed as candlepins. "We want to show respect," he said. "But we want to have fun with it, too." (Photograph by author.)

Candlepin bowling has survived two world wars, the Great Depression, and evolving consumer preferences. Adapting to these social and cultural changes requires commitment, creativity, and passion for the game. The candlepin houses that have responded to the current marketplace are thriving, and their customers keep coming back. "Candlepin players are loyal," said Maria Angelotti, executive director of the International Candlepin Bowling Association. "The game is in their blood." (Photograph by author.)

ABOUT THE AUTHOR

Blame the neon.

I am Susan Mara Bregman, a Boston-based author and photographer.

While researching my first book, *New England Neon*, I encountered neon signs for bowling in all its variations—tenpins, duckpins, and candlepins.

The next thing I knew, I picked up one of those small balls and felt a connection with another piece of New England history.

I looked beyond the signs to begin photographing the lanes, and this adventure began. New England has already lost too many candlepin houses—one closed while I was writing this—and I hope this book brings the story of this fun, challenging, and exasperating sport to current players and new audiences.

Outside the lanes, my portfolio and blog are online at www.rednickel.com, and I post on Instagram and Facebook as @RedNickelNeon.

DISCOVER THOUSANDS OF LOCAL HISTORY BOOKS FEATURING MILLIONS OF VINTAGE IMAGES

Arcadia Publishing, the leading local history publisher in the United States, is committed to making history accessible and meaningful through publishing books that celebrate and preserve the heritage of America's people and places.

Find more books like this at
www.arcadiapublishing.com

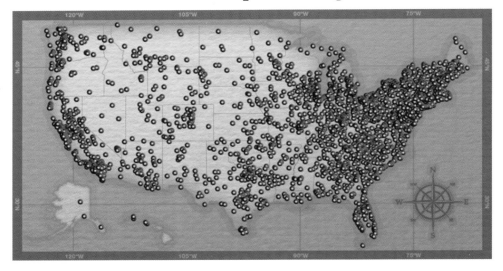

Search for your hometown history, your old stomping grounds, and even your favorite sports team.